Founded in 1895 by company in the wor legacy. Gaumont co as operate hundred library in Paris con to today, including comedies, footage and cultural figure

rious
ell
lm
1895
cal

The scene reproduced decades of the 20th century, as community halls all over France were converted into film houses, and film screenings became popular. In these film houses, live acts and orchestral performances were interspersed with full-length features, documentaries, newsreels, and short films.

GW00585954

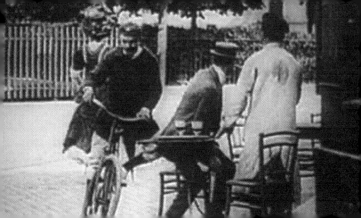